First Facts®

Mae Jemison

A 4D BOOK

by Mary Boone

CAPSTONE PRESS
a capstone imprint

This is a Capstone 4D book!

Want fun videos that go with this book?

Just visit www.capstone4d.com

Use this password
jemison.27742

First Facts are published by Capstone Press
1710 Roe Crest Drive, North Mankato, Minnesota 56003
www.mycapstone.com

Library of Congress Cataloging-in-Publication Data
Names: Boone, Mary, 1963– author.
Title: Mae Jemison / by Mary Boone.
Description: North Mankato, Minnesota : Capstone
Press, [2019] | Series: First facts. STEM scientists and
inventors | Series: A 4D book |
Audience: Ages 6–9. | Includes bibliographical
references and index.
Identifiers: LCCN 2018001967 (print) | LCCN 2018005842
(ebook) | ISBN 9781543527827 (eBook pdf) | ISBN
9781543527742 (hardcover) | ISBN 9781543527780 (pbk.)

Subjects: LCSH: Jemison, Mae, 1956—Juvenile literature.
| African American women astronauts—Biography—
Juvenile literature. | Astronauts—United States—
Biography—Juvenile literature.
Classification: LCC TL789.85.J46 (ebook) | LCC TL789.85.
J46 B66 2019 (print) | DDC 629.450092 [B] —dc23
LC record available at https://lccn.loc.gov/2018001967

Editorial Credits
Erika L. Shores and Jessica Server, editors;
Charmaine Whitman, designer; Eric Gohl, media
researcher; Laura Manthe, production specialist

Image Credits
AP Photo: 17, Mike Fisher, 9; Getty Images: Afro
Newspaper/Gado, cover, Bettmann, 13, 15, Corbis, 19,
Gary Gershoff, 21; iStockphoto: stevegeer, 7; NASA: 5, 18;
Shutterstock: Diego Grandi, 11, Zia Liu, cover & interior
(backgrounds)

Table of Contents

CHAPTER 1

Early Dreams

As a child, Mae Jemison enjoyed studying the night sky. She dreamed about going to the stars. When Mae grew up, those dreams came true. She became the first African American woman in space.

"What we find is that if you have a goal that is very, very far out, and you approach it in little steps, you start to get there faster. Your mind opens up to the possibilities."

Mae Jemison

Mae Jemison floats in space on board the space shuttle *Endeavour* in 1992.

Mae was born October 17, 1956, in Decatur, Alabama. Her father, Charlie, was a carpenter. Her mother, Dorothy, was a teacher. Mae is the youngest of three children. She has an older brother and an older sister. When Mae was 3, her family moved to Chicago.

Mae's high school in Chicago

Mae was a good student. She
spent many hours in the library.
She liked learning about the earth
and space. Her parents **supported**
her goal to become a scientist.
But some of her teachers did not.
One teacher told her girls should
be nurses.

support—to help and
encourage someone

In October 1992, Mae attended a ceremony at her former school in Chicago, Morgan Park High School.

Mae **graduated** from high school at age 16. She earned a **scholarship** to Stanford University. At Stanford, she was in dance and theater. Mae studied chemical **engineering** and African American studies. She then went to Cornell Medical College.

Dancing

Mae began taking dance classes when she was 11. She kept dancing in college. In her last year of college, she had to decide to become a doctor or become a dancer. Her mother told her, "You can always dance if you're a doctor, but you can't doctor if you're a dancer."

graduate—to finish all the required classes at school

scholarship—a grant or prize that pays for a student to go to college

engineering—using science to design and build things

FACT When Mae was in college she learned to speak Russian and Swahili.

Mae attended Stanford University in Palo Alto, California.

CHAPTER 2

Becoming Dr. Jemison

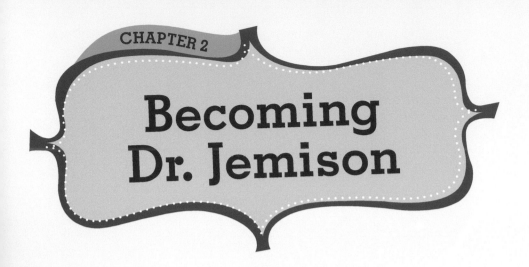

While going to medical school, Mae spent time studying in Cuba and Kenya. She also worked at a **refugee** camp in Thailand. Shortly after becoming a doctor, she joined the **Peace Corps**. She cared for the people of Sierra Leone and Liberia in Africa.

refugee—a person forced to leave his or her home or country to seek safety somewhere else

Peace Corps—an organization of trained volunteers from the United States that helps people in other countries; Peace Corps volunteers often help people with farming and education

Mae worked as a doctor in California after her time in the Peace Corps.

Mae returned to the United States in 1985. She wanted a change. She had long wanted to travel to space. Mae decided to **apply** to join NASA's astronaut training program. Nearly 2,000 people applied, but only 15 were chosen. Mae was one of these people.

Disaster In 1986 the space shuttle *Challenger* blew up after liftoff. All seven on board were killed. The disaster caused NASA to stop all missions for a time. Mae had applied to NASA before the disaster, and she applied again after it. She knew the danger. But she still wanted to go into space.

apply—to ask for something in writing

Reporters interviewed Mae while she toured NASA's Johnson Space Center in 1987.

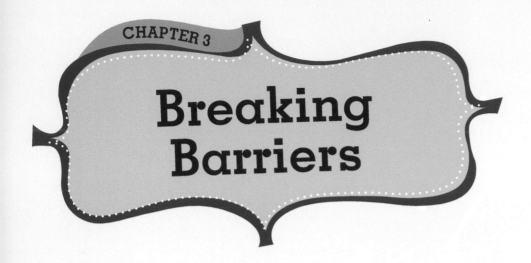

CHAPTER 3

Breaking Barriers

On June 4, 1987, Mae became the first African American woman chosen for the U.S. astronaut program. She would become a **mission** specialist. She learned how to do science experiments while in space.

mission—a planned task or job

Mae sat inside the space shuttle during her tour of Johnson Space Center in 1987.

Mae trained for more than four years. On September 12, 1992, she became the first African American woman in space. She and six other astronauts spent eight days on *Endeavour*. After her flight, she often spoke about what women and **minorities** can achieve.

Mae prepares to go into space.

minority—a group that makes up less than half of a large group

Mae (far right) and the six other *Endeavour* crew members

In March 1993, Mae left her job at NASA. She began teaching medicine at Dartmouth College. She also started a research company called The Jemison Group. She often gives speeches about science and its importance. Mae continues to share her work and knowledge in new ways.

A Star Among Stars

When Mae was a young girl, she liked the TV show *Star Trek*. When *Star Trek* actors found out Mae was a fan, they asked her to be on the show. In 1993, she played Lt. Palmer in an episode of *Star Trek: The Next Generation*.

FACT In 2001 Mae wrote a book about her life. It is called *Find Where the Wind Goes: Moments from My Life*.

Glossary

apply (uh-PLYE)—to ask for something in writing

engineering (en-juh-NEER-ing)—using science to design and build things

graduate (GRAJ-oo-ayt)—to finish all the required classes at a school

minority (MYE-nor-i-tee)—a group that makes up less than half of a large group

mission (MISH-uhn)—a planned task or job

Peace Corps (PEESS COR)—an organization of trained volunteers from the United States that helps people in other countries; Peace Corps volunteers often help people with farming and education

refugee (ref-yuh-JEE)—a person forced to leave his or her home or country to seek safety somewhere else

scholarship (SKOL-ur-ship)—a grant or prize that pays for a student to go to college

support (SUH-port)—to help and encourage someone

Read More

Barghoorn, Linda. *Mae Jemison: Trailblazing Astronaut, Doctor, and Teacher*. Remarkable Lives Revealed. Saint Catharines, Ont.: Crabtree Publishing, 2016.

Calkhoven, Laurie. *You Should Meet Mae Jemison*. New York: Simon Spotlight, 2016.

Lassieur, Allison. *Astronaut Mae Jemison*. STEM Trailblazer Bios. New York: Lerner Classroom, 2016.

Internet Sites

Use Facthound to find Internet sites related to this book.

Visit *www.facthound.com*

Just type in 9781543527742 and go!

Check out projects, games and lots more at
www.capstonekids.com

Critical Thinking Questions

1. What was Mae's training like to travel to space?

2. If you could ask an astronaut any question, what would you ask?

3. Mae had to choose between becoming a doctor or becoming a dancer. Do you think she made a good choice? Why or why not?

Index